HUBBLE AND THE BIG BANG

PAUL KUPPERBERG

rosen central
Primary Source™

The Rosen Publishing Group, Inc., New York

Published in 2005 by The Rosen Publishing Group, Inc.
29 East 21st Street, New York, NY 10010

Library of Congress Cataloging-in-Publication Data

Kupperberg, Paul.
Hubble and the Big Bang / Paul Kupperberg.— 1st ed.
p. cm. — (Primary sources of revolutionary scientific discoveries and theories)
Includes bibliographical references and index.
ISBN 1-4042-0307-9 (lib. bdg.)
1. Hubble, Edwin Powell, 1889–1953—Juvenile literature. 2. Big bang theory—Juvenile literature. 3. Astronomers—United States—Biography—Juvenile literature.
I. Title. II. Series.
QB36.H83K87 2005
520'.92—dc22

2004007793

Printed in Hong Kong

On the front cover: Photograph of Edwin Hubble

On the back cover: Top to bottom: Nicolaus Copernicus, Charles Darwin, Edwin Hubble, Johannes Kepler, Gregor Mendel, Dmitry Mendeleyev, Isaac Newton, James Watson *(right)* and Francis Crick *(left)*

ONTENTS

INTRODUCTION

A long time ago, man thought that he was alone at the center of an unchanging universe. The Sun, he believed, revolved around Earth, and all the stars were part of a bubble that encircled the cosmos. Man's understanding of the universe came into focus slowly. Scientists such as Copernicus, Kepler, Galileo, Newton, and Einstein contributed to the science of cosmology, the study of the universe.

THE EXPANDING UNIVERSE

In the span of the last century, mankind's knowledge of space and the complex laws of physics that govern it has grown larger and faster than ever before in history. Scientists and astronomers who study the deepest reaches of space have discovered a great number of wonders that earlier scientists could never have imagined, from quasars and pulsars to black holes and planets orbiting distant suns.

Yet among scientists, few discoveries were as important as those made by American scientist Edwin Powell Hubble in the 1920s. Before Hubble pointed the telescopes of the University of Chicago's Yerkes Observatory toward the night skies, most scientists believed that our galaxy, the Milky Way, which is 100,000 light-years across, was all there was to the universe. Hubble showed us that the Milky Way was but one of millions of such galaxies filling a space larger than anyone had ever

Shown here in this 1999 photograph is the Yerkes refractor telescope inside the dome of the Yerkes Observatory in Williams Bay, Wisconsin. The 40-inch (102 cm) telescope is the largest refractor telescope in the world, as it was back in Hubble's day. This is where Hubble first began to study the heavens. Studying under George Ellery Hale, head of the astronomy department at the University of Chicago and creator of the telescope, Hubble used this telescope to make the observations that would eventually lead to his theories of the big bang and the expanding universe.

before imagined. He also determined that the cosmos is expanding, inflating like a gigantic balloon.

Such an expansion, equal in its speed and growth in all directions across space, could only be the result of an "explosion" at the beginning of time. Though it is often referred to as an explosion, we must remember that this "explosion" was the beginning of the universe itself. The universe didn't "explode" in the way a bomb explodes, because there was nothing for it to explode within—nothing yet existed. We use the term, however, for simplicity's sake when describing the beginning of the universe.

Named by British scientist Fred Hoyle, this "explosion" came to be known as the big bang. The big bang was the instant when all the matter in the universe, which had been packed into a single, incredibly dense sphere, exploded. This explosion is believed to have unleashed the materials that would become the countless stars and planets and bodies that now inhabit the universe.

In short, Edwin Hubble was responsible for discovering the size of the universe and that it is expanding. Though he was careful in his papers to avoid drawing conclusions about why the universe was expanding, Hubble's discovery forced scientists to change their basic view of the cosmos. Even the brilliant physicist Albert Einstein was moved by Hubble's discovery. After Edwin Hubble, our ideas about the universe have never been the same.

CHAPTER 1

HUBBLE BEFORE COSMOLOGY

Edwin Hubble's fascination with the skies began at an early age, at a time when people believed that the universe was much smaller than the size they now believe it to be. It was the summer of 1897 when the seven-year-old boy had his first look at the heavens. Edwin's grandfather, William Henderson James, of Springfield, Missouri, owned a small telescope that he kept set up in his backyard. During a summer visit, Edwin spent hours in the evenings peering through the amazing device, watching the progress of celestial objects as they moved across the night sky. He was so fascinated by what he saw that he had only one present in mind for his upcoming eighth birthday on November 20 of that year: to spend the entire night, from dusk to dawn, observing the heavens through the lens of his grandfather's telescope.

Having dressed warmly and filled his pockets with a sandwich and cookies to sustain him through the night, Edwin positioned himself at the telescope's eyepiece and began his all-night watch. That evening the sky was perfectly clear, lit only by a sliver of the crescent moon and the twinkle of the countless stars that dotted the darkness. Edwin kept watch throughout the night, determined not to miss a moment of the astonishing show that passed before the lens of his telescope.

Little more than twenty-seven years to the day later, on November 24, 1924, that same dogged determination would bring Edwin Hubble to the attention of the world as the man who would forever change mankind's concept of the universe and our place in it.

The Young Scholar

On November 20, 1889, fourteen years before the Wright brothers flew the first airplane at Kitty Hawk, North Carolina, and seven years before Henry Ford produced his first automobile in Detroit, Michigan, Edwin Powell Hubble was born. Edwin was born in Marshfield, Missouri, to John and Virginia Lee James Hubble, a well-to-do Missouri family. He was the third of nine Hubble children.

Though John Hubble had studied law, he joined the family's insurance business. This forced his growing family to move to Springfield, Missouri, where the headquarters of the insurance company he worked for was located. They then moved to the suburbs of Chicago, Illinois, first in Evanston and, finally, to Wheaton.

The Hubbles were a close-knit family, watched over by a stern father and a tolerant mother. Both parents taught their children a strong sense of family and responsibility. Edwin was an avid reader of adventure novels, including the fantastic tales of pioneer science-fiction writers Jules Verne and H. Rider Haggard.

But while Edwin and his siblings lived a fairly easy and happy life, his childhood was not without tragedy. His younger

Edwin Hubble's fascination with the heavens can arguably be attributed to the books he read as a child. Shown here are fantastic illustrations in the book *Round the Moon* by Jules Verne, who was one of Hubble's favorite science-fiction authors. One of the pioneers of science-fiction writing, Verne wrote stories that involved space adventure and exploration. Hubble surely found the inspiration from these books to embark on his own scientific exploration of the universe.

sister Virginia died of scarlet fever not long after she and Edwin had an argument. He was shattered by her death, taking to his room for a month afterward, only to emerge a changed young man. He became much more serious, taking on the added responsibility of watching over the rest of his younger brothers and sisters.

Edwin's introduction to astronomy in 1897 would have a lasting impact on his life. He shared his interest with his grandfather

William Henderson James, to whom, at age twelve, he wrote a letter that predicted the possibility of life on Mars.

Edwin was an imaginative and talented student who seemed able to get good grades with little effort. He graduated from high school in 1906 and was awarded a scholarship to the University of Chicago for his academic achievements.

From Chicago to Oxford

Edwin Hubble came to the University of Chicago at a time when it was home to a number of eminent astronomers and physicists. In addition, the university housed the Yerkes Observatory in Williams Bay, Wisconsin. The observatory then, as now, contained the largest refractor telescope in the world. In 1897, the 40-inch (102-centimeter) telescope was created by the pioneer astrophysicist George Ellery Hale (1868–1938), head of the astronomy department at the university.

Majoring in mathematics and astronomy, Hubble studied under such leading scientists as Professor Hale. Hubble also had access to the magnificent telescope there. While he had been free to observe whatever he wished as an eight-year-old through his grandfather's small telescope, time on the giant Yerkes was precious. It was booked for specific projects, mostly solar observations, which was Hale's area of specialization. Hubble worked on one of Hale's projects, the study and photographing of the Sun during its active sunspot cycles.

In September 1910, Edwin Hubble graduated from the University of Chicago and was awarded a Rhodes scholarship for postgraduate study at Oxford university in England. This scholarship is given to students with superior academic records who also excel in sports and display good character traits.

Champions of the West.

Edwin Hubble arrived at the University of Chicago as an undergraduate in 1906. Shown here is a photograph of Hubble with his University of Chicago basketball team in 1910. During his four years in attendance at the university, he would engage in study that would put him in contact with some of the leading astronomers of the day, including George Ellery Hale, who headed the astronomy department of the university.

Concerned that he might not be able to make an adequate living in mathematics and astronomy, Hubble chose not to pursue his scientific studies. Instead, he enrolled in Oxford University's Queen's College to study law. The young American made the most of his three years at Oxford, spending his summers traveling through Germany, France, and Switzerland.

Returning Home

At the end of his three years abroad, Hubble returned home with a bachelor's degree. He taught high school Spanish and physics, translated documents from German to English, and even worked with a group of surveyors mapping a railroad line through the northern Wisconsin wilderness.

By the spring of 1914, Hubble had apparently reached a decision about what he wanted to do with his life. He wrote to Forest Ray Moulton, his former teacher at the University of Chicago, to apply as a graduate student. Edwin R. Frost, the director of the Yerkes Observatory, accepted Hubble and arranged for the returning student to receive a scholarship. He also invited Hubble to accompany him to a meeting of the American Astronomical Society at Northwestern University in Evanston, Illinois, in August 1914.

It was at the meeting—where Hubble was elected a member of the prestigious organization—that Hubble first became interested in the mysterious objects in the farthest reaches of space. Astronomers called these objects nebulae (from the Latin word *nebula*, or "cloud").

There were two types of nebulae recognized during this period. The first was a formation of clouds, dust, and gas. The second was a faint, fuzzy object that was spiral in shape. This was known as a spiral nebula. Spiral nebulae are flattened, rotating disks of groups of young stars, with a central bulge and a surrounding halo of older stars. They also contain dense groups of old stars called globular clusters, which were Hubble's own area of specialty. The nature of spiral nebulae was uncertain at the time, though. Some astronomers thought they were made of collections of stars outside the Milky Way. Other astronomers thought they were collections of faint stars and gas within the Milky Way.

Nebulae in general appeared to observers on Earth as though they were not moving. But a paper delivered by American astronomer Dr. Vesto M. Slipher (1875–1969) presented photographic evidence that proved otherwise. The evidence seemed to show that thirteen nebulae were receding, or moving away, from Earth at incredibly high speeds through space. Dr. Slipher's radical theory and calculations were dismissed by many of his fellow astronomers as sloppy research. But Hubble was intrigued by the scientific puzzle over whether the nebulae were in fact receding.

Beginning His Research

At the Yerkes Observatory's smaller 24-inch (61 cm) telescope, Hubble set out to photograph distant stars in spiral nebulae that seemed to be moving away from Earth. By comparing his photographic plates against those made of the same section of the sky a decade earlier, he discovered a dozen stars whose light followed similar varied patterns. He concluded that these objects were the faintest stars in which any motion had been found. But recalling the hostile reception to Dr. Slipher's controversial findings, Hubble was hesitant to go public with his conclusions until he could prove his theory.

The study of spiral nebulae was still new and their origin and composition were unknown. The answer to the mystery of their movement depended on how far from Earth they were located. If, as was believed at the time, the entire universe was only a few thousand light-years across, the spiral nebulae's makeup was most likely collections of glowing interstellar dust and gas, lit from behind by even more distant stars. But if, as Hubble supposed, the universe was far larger than believed, these cloudy smudges against the blackness of space might just be clusters of galaxies, star systems at distances of millions of light-years.

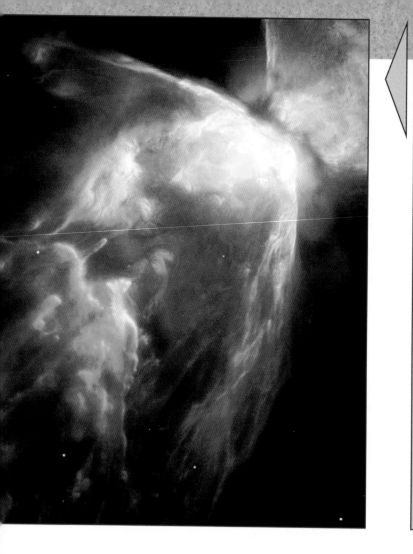

Hubble began his career studying nebulae like the Bug Nebula (NGC 6302) shown here. His observation that nebulae were moving outward became the basis for his theory that the universe is expanding. This image was released in 2004 and was taken by the most powerful telescope in the world, the aptly named Hubble Space Telescope. A dark ring surrounds the inner nebula, shown at the upper right. At the center of it all is one of the hottest stars known. Despite temperatures of at least 450,032° Fahrenheit (250,000° Celsius), the star has never been seen. It is hidden behind the blanket of nebula dust, but the telescope can still detect its radiation.

Hubble finished his doctoral dissertation, "Photographic Investigations of Faint Nebulae," in 1917. He was a newcomer to the study of nebulae, which was itself a new field of study. Although nearly 2,000 nebulae had so far been discovered, they could not yet be positively identified as being made of stars. But Hubble had taken the first step on the road to identifying what spiral nebulae were. More important, Hubble led the way to understanding their place in the creation of the universe.

HAPTER 2

Mankind has always looked to the skies in wonder and awe. For most of human history, the movements of the heavenly bodies remained a mystery to earthbound observers. It was commonly believed that Earth stood stationary at the center of a celestial sphere around which the Sun and planets revolved through space between us and the stars, themselves fixed points of light on the sphere's interior wall.

COSMOLOGY BEFORE HUBBLE

The ancient Greeks from the fourth century BC were the first civilization to develop a cosmological model of the universe. This cosmological model was a general scientific philosophy that tried to explain the universe. It did this by interpreting and explaining the movements of the planets and other celestial bodies across the night sky.

Lacking the ability to closely observe the cosmos, and without enough knowledge of the cosmos to conceive of a wider universe that did not have man and his world at the center of everything, the Greeks placed Earth at the center of the universe around which all else revolved. So, in the second century AD, the Greek philosopher and mathematician Ptolemy came up with the geocentric (Earth-centered) cosmological theory. This came to be known as the Ptolemaic system.

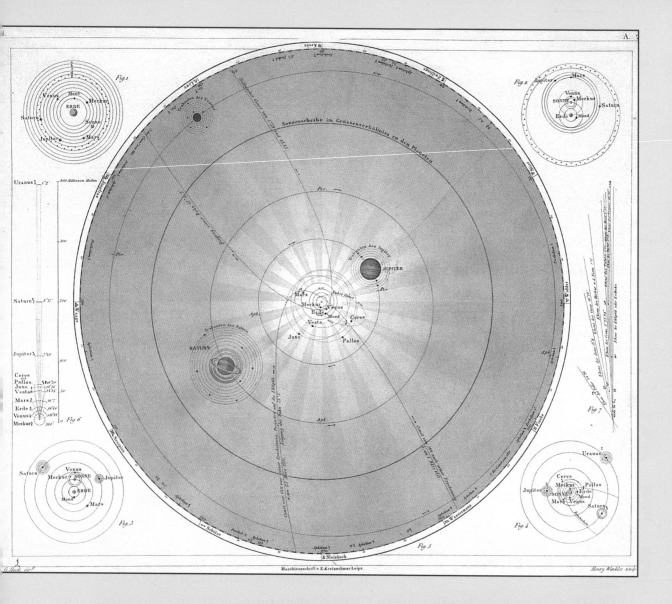

Throughout history, there have been many models of how the universe is structured. This diagram from *Bilder Atlas* (1860), by Johann Georg Heck, shows the various models proposed over the years. The main diagram at the center is of the heliocentric (Sun-centered) universe, containing only the then-known six planets, their satellites, and other celestial bodies orbiting the Sun. At the upper left is the geocentric (Earth-centered) Ptolemaic model from the second century AD. The Ptolemaic model, however, was overthrown by the model at the lower right, the heliocentric Copernican model of 1543. The Egyptian model at the lower left and Tychonic model at the upper right were both also geocentric.

There was one problem. Planets are generally seen to be moving from east to west as observed against the background stars. Occasionally, though, they appear to reverse direction. They appear to move from west to east, only to slow down, and reverse direction again back to their usual east to west motion. Why didn't the planets move in normal, uninterrupted paths across the sky like the stars did?

This apparent change in motion is due to the fact that the planets, including Earth, revolve around the Sun, and that the farther away a planet is from the Sun, the slower it moves in its orbit. From our perspective on Earth, planets that appear to change direction are actually moving slower in their orbits than Earth is. Earth, in effect, "laps" those planets as a runner on a racetrack would lap a slower runner.

Ptolemy explained this strange phenomenon by using the concept of epicycles. Epicycles explained that each planet moved in circles upon circles around the fixed Earth. Though it was complicated, the Ptolemaic system was sufficient for the time at explaining the movement of the planets and stood unchallenged for some 1,400 years.

The Ptolemaic system was challenged when the Polish astronomer Nicolaus Copernicus (1473–1543) introduced his own heliocentric model of the solar system in 1512, though it wasn't officially published until 1543. In the Copernican model, Earth and the other planets rotated on their own axes while moving in circular orbits around the Sun.

Like other astronomers of the time, however, the Danish astronomer Tycho Brahe (1546–1601) rejected Copernicus's theory. Brahe thought that if Earth were moving around the Sun, then the stars in the sky would appear to be in different

Tycho Brahe, shown here, was one of the more colorful scientists in history who came before Hubble. Always quarrelsome, his nose was partially severed as the result of a duel he had with one of his students over a mathematical disagreement. After the match, he was seen wearing a gold and silver replacement nose, which he continually polished. Brahe was better known for his unique model of the universe, which rejected the Copernican heliocentric theory, claiming that Earth, instead, is the center of the universe. Along with Copernicus, Galileo, and Newton, Brahe was one of the pioneers in the study of how the universe is structured. These pioneers paved the way for Edwin Hubble.

positions as Earth made its way around its orbit. This apparent change in the position of an object when viewed against a background from different vantage points is known as parallax. Another example of parallax is the apparent change in position of your thumb when you hold it out in front of you against a stationary background and view it with one eye closed, and then the other.

But to Brahe, the stars appeared to have fixed positions in the sky no matter when they were viewed throughout the year. With no evidence of parallax to be found, Brahe believed that either Earth was the center of the universe or the stars were so far away that parallax wouldn't be noticeable. But this latter theory was one that seventeenth-century science was not yet willing to accept.

A Variety of Discoveries

It would fall to the Italian scientist Galileo Galilei (1564–1642) to offer proof of the heliocentric model of the solar system. Using a new invention from Denmark called the telescope, Galileo discovered moons orbiting the planet Jupiter. If a moon could orbit a planet, he reasoned, then a planet could orbit the Sun. His 1632 work, *Dialogue Concerning the Two Chief World Systems*, argued for the Copernican system. The publication of the book proved to be a turning point in astronomical thought.

Around this time, the German astronomer Johannes Kepler (1571–1630) was developing a series of laws, or mathematical proofs, that upheld the heliocentric model. By studying the orbit of Mars, he realized that the planets not only orbit the Sun, but that they orbit in elliptical paths. Because the planets' orbits are ellipses, the Sun is not at the exact center of their orbits. This means that during its orbital cycle, a planet will sometimes be closer to the Sun than at other times.

Kepler showed that a planet moves faster when it is nearer the Sun and slower when it is farther from the Sun. Also, the farther from the Sun a planet's orbit is, the longer it takes to orbit. So Mercury, the planet closest to the Sun, makes a single orbit in 88 days, while Pluto, farthest from the Sun, requires 248 years. This was a groundbreaking discovery.

Then in 1687, the English mathematician and physicist Isaac Newton (1642–1727) published his *Philosophiae Naturalis Principia Mathematica* (Mathematical Principles of Natural Philosophy). This landmark work covered a breathtaking range of new theories in physics and mathematics. It also included Newton's theories on gravity.

Gravity is the force of attraction between all masses in the universe, such as the attraction of Earth's mass for bodies near its surface. Newton said that gravitation between two bodies is proportional to their masses and inversely proportional to the square of the distance between them. By identifying and describing the force of gravitation, Newton's theory explained Kepler's laws governing the motions of the planets and all other celestial bodies by explaining the forces that make them work.

Adding to Newton's discoveries, German philosopher Immanuel Kant (1724–1804) proposed that the Milky Way was but one of a number of "island universes," or galaxies. Beyond our Milky Way must be other galaxies, perhaps an infinite number of them. Still, the belief that the Milky Way made up the whole universe persisted.

But the German astronomer and mathematician Friedrich Wilhelm Bessel (1784–1846) finally put to rest the mystery of parallax when he measured the distance of the star 61 Cygni from Earth in 1838. He determined its distance to be approximately 25 million, million miles from Earth. In contrast, Earth orbits about 93 million miles from the Sun.

The true nature of the spiral nebulae and the universe was waiting only for a man like Edwin Hubble to come along. By patiently observing spiral nebulae through the lens of the most powerful telescopes in the world, he finally saw for himself how the universe had been constructed.

CHAPTER 3

HUBBLE'S UNIVERSE

The day after finishing his doctoral thesis, Edwin Hubble joined the United States Army. In April 1917, America had entered World War I, which had been raging for three years in Europe. Hubble felt strongly that he had no choice but to help fight the war against Germany and its allies.

Just before enlisting, the twenty-eight-year-old received an invitation from his former University of Chicago professor, George Ellery Hale, to join Hale's staff at the newly completed Mount Wilson Observatory. The observatory was part of the California Institute of Technology (Cal Tech). But Hubble sent Hale his reluctant regrets about not being able to join him and reported instead to Officer's Training Camp at Fort Sheridan, Illinois.

After training, Captain Hubble was placed in charge of training new recruits assigned to the newly formed 85th Black Hawk Division. By December 1917, he was promoted to major in command of the 2nd Battalion of the 343rd Infantry. Major Hubble shipped out to Europe in September 1918. Though willing to do his part in combat, he had arrived too late. On November 11, 1918, World War I ended. It would take Hubble nine months, however, to return home to the States and be released from the military. Hubble headed

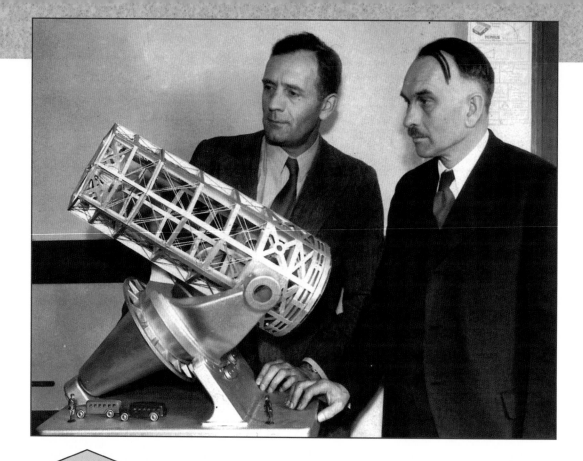

Edwin Hubble (*left*) and mathematician Dr. Richard Chase Tolman are shown here observing a model of a new 200-inch telescope. This telescope would eventually be known as the Hale Telescope in Mount Palomar, California, named after noted astrophysicist George Ellery Hale, under whom Hubble studied. The model was displayed at the summer session of the American Association for the Advancement of Science in Pasadena, California. Dedicated on June 3, 1948, the telescope was used by Hubble to take the first photographic plate, which was of a variable nebula.

directly for Pasadena, California, where Professor Hale still had an opening for the promising new astronomer at the Mount Wilson Observatory.

Spiral Nebulae

When Edwin Hubble and George Hale had last worked together, Hale had mainly been interested in the study of the Sun. Since then, however, he had become intrigued by spiral nebulae.

Shown here are galaxy M31 (the Andromeda galaxy) and galaxy M33 (the Triangulum galaxy). Hubble used Cepheid variable stars within these galaxies to prove that galaxies other than the Milky Way existed in the universe. Using Cepheids, Hubble was also able to determine that the universe is much larger than previously thought. He calculated the size of the universe by using the Cepheids to measure how far away distant galaxies were. Through his calculations he learned that galaxies existed many times farther away than had ever before been imagined. From his studies using Cepheid variable stars, Hubble was ultimately able to build the foundation for his theories of the big bang and the expanding universe.

Hubble sought to measure the distance to specific spiral nebulae to determine if they fell within our own galaxy. He could then compare those measurements to those of objects he believed to be millions of light-years farther away. He was also curious to learn if these nebulae were stationary or receding from Earth.

He began his studies by photographing a large area of the night sky as far from Earth as Mount Wilson's giant Hooker Telescope could see. Night after night, he sat at the telescope exposing photographic plates until he knew the sky and its countless stars as intimately as another man might know the layout of his own home.

Measuring the cosmic distances between stars was then, as today, no simple task. In 1912, Henrietta Swan Leavitt, an astronomer at the Harvard College Observatory in Cambridge, Massachusetts, had observed that certain stars varied in their brightness, changing from bright to dim and back, or pulsating. These stars, as we know now, have used up their main supply of hydrogen fuel. This makes them unstable and causes them to pulsate. They are called Cepheid variable stars, named after the constellation Cepheus in which the first one was discovered. The length of a Cepheid's cycle from dim to bright determined its average luminosity, or the average amount of light it gave off. So a Cepheid with a particular brightness cycle closer to Earth gave off the same amount of light as one with an identical cycle farther away from Earth. This is true no matter where in space the Cepheid is located.

By knowing the distance to the closer Cepheid, it is possible to find the distance to a farther Cepheid. This is done through a calculation based on the fact that the object appears dimmer the farther away the observer is from it. How bright an object appears to be decreases the farther away it is. Specifically, the brightness decreases in proportion to the square of the distance between the star and the observer. So, for objects with the same brightness, an object that appears one ten-thousandth as bright as another would have to be 100 times farther away. This is how the distances of Cepheids were calculated.

By the time Hubble was making his observations, another Mount Wilson astronomer, Harlow Shapley (1885–1972), had already measured the size of the Milky Way. Like Hubble, Shapley used Cepheids to make his measurements of globular clusters around the Milky Way. From this, he calculated our galaxy to be some 300,000 light-years across. This was 100 times larger than had been previously figured.

Shapley was convinced that the Milky Way comprised the entire universe. He was one of the most vocal critics of the so-called island universe theory put forth by Kant and others since the nineteenth century. The nebulae that so intrigued Hubble, Shapley insisted, were nothing more than relatively nearby clouds of glowing gas.

"VAR!"

Hubble believed otherwise, and by October 6, 1923, he had found the proof that would convince the rest of the scientific community. Hubble discovered a Cepheid variable in the Andromeda nebula, one of the distant spiral nebulae he had been observing through the Mount Wilson telescope. A single photographic plate of Andromeda (officially classified as M31) showed the Cepheid. This was labeled in Hubble's own hand as "VAR!" and was the linchpin of his remarkable discovery. It appeared to be much fainter than those closer Cepheids with the same cycle, so he knew it was much farther away.

Hubble's calculations were startling, showing that the faint patch of light was actually 100,000 times, or nearly 1 million light-years, farther away from Earth than even the nearest stars! If, as Harlow Shapley believed, our galaxy was some 300,000 light-years across, the 1 million light-year distant Andromeda nebula could not possibly lie within the Milky Way.

Hubble now had evidence of the island universe theory. The Milky Way, as large as it may have seemed, was not the whole universe. It was, in fact, a galaxy, a cluster of gas, dust, and billions of

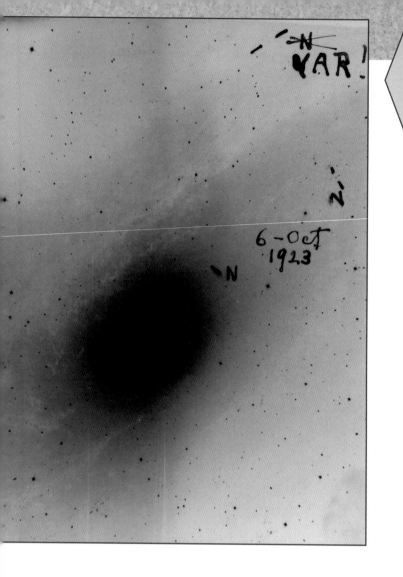

On October 6, 1923, Hubble discovered the evidence that would prove Immanuel Kant's island universe theory. Named simply "VAR!" on the photographic plate he detected it with, shown here, the Cepheid variable star in the Andromeda nebula would prove that there were galaxies that existed beyond our own Milky Way. Cepheids were key to Hubble's theories on the size and expansion of the universe. By measuring their radiation, Hubble could determine how far away they were. With his discovery of the Cepheid in the Andromeda nebula, Hubble was able to prove that the Andromeda nebula was hundreds of thousands of light-years beyond the edge of the Milky Way. This discovery opened up a universe of possibilities for Hubble.

stars that were held together by gravitational attraction. As we were eventually to learn, it was one of tens of billions of similar galaxies spread across an unimaginably huge universe. Andromeda was only our nearest neighbor! Thanks to Edwin Hubble's discovery, the island universe theory was a theory no longer.

Hubble would develop other methods for measuring distances to galaxies similar to Leavitt's Cepheid method. These methods, however, were based on studies done on spiral galaxies instead of individual stars. Galaxies of the same general shape, appearance, and speed of rotation observed through the same telescope must, he concluded, be similar in size to one another even if one appears larger than the other. The galaxy that looks larger might appear 100

This article was published in the *New York Times* on November 22, 1924. It announces Hubble's discovery that confirmed Immanuel Kant's island universe theory that galaxies exist beyond our own. This breakthrough was the first step for Hubble on the road to discovering the size of the universe and the big bang theory. As a result of his discovery, Hubble became an instant celebrity. The dedicated scientist didn't let fame interfere with his studies, though. He pursued other theories he had, including a classification system for newly discovered galaxies. In the end, though, his discovery of "VAR!" was the foundation for his greatest achievements. (See page 53 for transcription.)

FINDS SPIRAL NEBULAE ARE STELLAR SYSTEMS

Dr. Hubbell Confirms View That They Are 'Island Universes' Similar to Our Own.

WASHINGTON, Nov. 22.—Confirmation of the view that the spiral nebulae, which appear in the heavens as whirling clouds, are in reality distant stellar systems, or "island universes," has been obtained by Dr. Edwin Hubbell of the Carnegie Institution's Mount Wilson observatory, through investigations carried out with the observatory's powerful telescopes.

The number of spiral nebulae, the observatory officials have reported to the institution, is very great, amounting to hundreds of thousands, and their apparent sizes range from small objects, almost star-like in character, to the great rebulae in Andromeda, which extends across an angle some 3 degrees in the heavens, about six times the diameter of the full moon.

"The investigations of Dr. Hubbell

times brighter than the smaller galaxy. But, as with Cepheids, that would mean that the seemingly smaller galaxy was ten times farther away than the seemingly larger one. Though only a rough estimate of the vast stretches of space between galaxies, Hubble's methods for calculating these distances are still in use.

On November 22, 1924, shortly after Hubble returned from an extended honeymoon in Europe, a headline in the *New York Times* read "Finds Spiral Nebulae are Stellar Systems. Doctor Hubbell [sic] Confirms View that they are 'Island Universes' similar to Our Own." The article reported Hubble's findings and made him an overnight celebrity. But the newly prominent astronomer had already set his sights on a new puzzle.

A Classification System

Hubble decided that the next step in his study of the universe was to develop a classification system for the newly discovered galaxies. He was assisted by Milton Humason, a man with an elementary school education who rose from janitor at the Mount Wilson Observatory to a position as assistant astronomer. He was now one of the leading experts in the field, eventually becoming an astronomer at the Mount Wilson and Palomar Observatories in California.

Together, they set out to photograph as many nebulae as they could, classifying them according to shape: elliptical, spiral, barred spiral, and, for those galaxies that conformed to no other categories, irregular. With these basic shapes, he introduced a system of classification that scientists use to this very day. Hubble presented this system, complete with photographic plates, in a paper in a 1926 issue of the *Astrophysical Journal*.

The Doppler Effect

Light from a star could be analyzed by looking at it through a device called a spectroscope. This instrument uses a prism, or a piece of triangular-shaped translucent glass or crystal, to separate light into the colors of the visible spectrum: red, orange, yellow, green, blue, indigo, and violet. The same principle of a spectrum is at work when sunlight passes through raindrops in the atmosphere, producing a rainbow.

By viewing the light from an object through a spectroscope, scientists can tell what an object is made of. The bands of colors, or spectral lines, represent different elements and compounds.

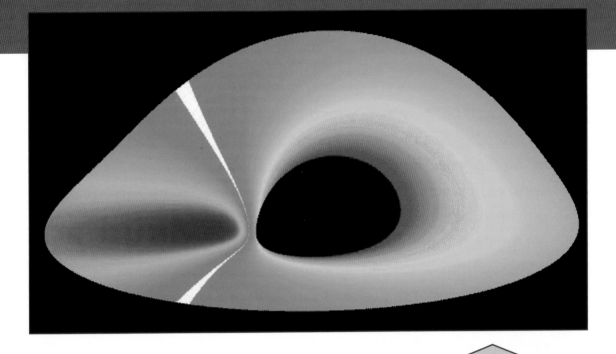

This is a virtual representation of the Doppler effect. Shown here is radiation surrounding a black hole, a region of space around a collapsed star with such strong gravitational force that not even light can escape it. The fact that light cannot escape a black hole is the reason why the center of this image is black, or absent of radiation. The area of radiation to the left of the white line is blueshifted. The blue shift indicates that the radiation is moving toward the observer. The area of radiation to the right of the white line is redshifted and moving away from the observer.

Thus, an observer on Earth can tell the chemical makeup of a star even hundreds of millions of light-years away.

By comparing the spectral lines of the light from stars in distant galaxies, Hubble saw that they matched those of many familiar elements, including helium, hydrogen, calcium, and titanium, all of which are present in our own Sun. The light from these distant stars also showed a consistent shift toward the red end of the spectrum, a phenomenon known as the Doppler effect.

The Doppler effect is a change in the wavelength and frequency of a wave. This change is a result of the motion of either the source of the wave (which can be either light or sound) or the receiver. For instance, we experience the Doppler effect in the case of an approaching fire truck siren. The sound it makes as it approaches gets higher, changing to a lower pitch once it passes us. This is because when the truck approaches us, the sound waves get pushed together, increasing the frequency, or the amount of waves within a certain amount of space. This makes the wavelengths shorter and increases the pitch of the siren. When the truck moves away from us, the wavelengths become longer and the frequency lowers, thus lowering the pitch.

With light, the effect of movement toward the receiver causes the frequency to increase and the wavelength to shorten because the waves are being pressed together as well. This shifting of the spectral lines toward the blue end of the spectrum is known as blueshift (blue wavelengths are the shorter wavelengths of the spectrum). When the source of light and the receiver are moving apart, the frequency decreases and the wavelength increases, making the light appear toward the red end of the spectrum, called redshift (red wavelengths are the longer wavelengths of the spectrum).

Knowing that the universe is expanding, Hubble was not surprised to find a redshift in his spectroscopic analysis of distant stars, indicating that they were moving away. Hubble determined the distances to galaxies using Cepheid variables. He also calculated how fast those galaxies were moving away from us by using the Doppler effect. With these two pieces of information, he found a relationship between the distance of the galaxies and how fast they were moving away from us—the farther away a galaxy is, the faster it is moving away. This relationship between distance and speed is called the Hubble constant. Some of the more distant objects he was able to observe were moving at speeds of up to 90 percent of the speed of light.

Origin of the Universe

German-born Albert Einstein (1879–1955) is considered perhaps the greatest physicist of all time. His special theory of relativity (1905) forever changed scientists' views of the universe. It linked time and space together. It also determined that the speed of light (186,282 mi/s [299,727 km/s]) was the same for everyone, everywhere, regardless of the motion of the observer or the source of the light.

Einstein knew that matter tends to fall together under gravity, making it seemingly impossible to have a static, or motionless, universe. Without some other force being exerted equally across the universe, the laws of physics said that it must either collapse upon itself or expand to escape gravity.

In order to explain the balance of gravitational forces, which keep the galaxies apart and the universe from collapsing, Einstein was forced to introduce an arbitrary calculation into his equations, a fictitious force pushing objects away from one another, which he called the "cosmological constant." The cosmological constant represented hypothetical energy in empty space that created the force that pushed objects in the universe away from each other.

Thanks to Hubble's remarkable discovery, Einstein was at last able to remove the arbitrarily inserted constant from his equations and accept Hubble's theory that the speed at which objects were traveling was directly related to their distance. This concept can be compared to an inflating balloon. Two spots on the balloon's surface will move apart faster as the balloon expands. In other words, a galaxy 100 million light-years away from Earth is receding from us twice as fast as a galaxy that is 50 million light-years away.

The Hubble constant, or Hubble's law, was published in the *Proceedings of the National Academy of Sciences* as "A Relation Between Distance and Radial Velocity Among Extra-Galactic Nebulae," and it became the cornerstone of what would become known as the big bang theory. Edwin Hubble had not only broadened our view of the universe, he had also led the way to discovering the nature of its very birth.

CHAPTER 4

For the Hubble constant to work as it does implies that the big bang theory is true. The first bits of matter flung outward in all directions by this "explosion" of creation would be the oldest, and thus the farthest, matter.

The Homogenous Universe

In 1922, Russian physicist and mathematician Alexander Friedmann (1888–1925), unwilling to accept Einstein's cosmological constant, theorized that objects in the universe

THE BIG BANG

are evenly distributed. This would be the case no matter where we were observing the universe from. On the cosmic scale, this means that the observation of distant galaxies in every direction shows there to be a more or less equal number of galaxies no matter where we look. This is not because we are at the center of the universe, but because there is an equal amount of mass spread evenly across the universe. So no matter what our location anywhere in the universe is, the amount of matter we see—that is, the number of visible stars and galaxies—should be more or less the same. Matter is therefore distributed evenly, or homogeneously, across the universe.

Not only did Friedmann's ideas presage Hubble's confirmation of the expanding universe in 1929, but it was a vital

Communications from the Mount Wilson Observatory, to the
NATIONAL ACADEMY OF SCIENCES, No. 105.

Reprinted from the Proceedings of the NATIONAL ACADEMY OF SCIENCES,
Vol. 15, No. 3, pp. 168-173. March, 1929.

A RELATION BETWEEN DISTANCE AND RADIAL VELOCITY AMONG EXTRA-GALACTIC NEBULAE

BY EDWIN HUBBLE

MOUNT WILSON OBSERVATORY, CARNEGIE INSTITUTION OF WASHINGTON

Communicated January 17, 1929

Determinations of the motion of the sun with respect to the extra-galactic nebulae have involved a K term of several hundred kilometers which appears to be variable. Explanations of this paradox have been sought in a correlation between apparent radial velocities and distances, but so far the results have not been convincing. The present paper is a re-examination of the question, based on only those nebular distances which are believed to be fairly reliable.

Distances of extra-galactic nebulae depend ultimately upon the application of absolute-luminosity criteria to involved stars whose types can be recognized. These include, among others, Cepheid variables, novae, and blue stars involved in emission nebulosity. Numerical values depend upon the zero point of the period-luminosity relation among Cepheids, the other criteria merely check the order of the distances. This method is restricted to the few nebulae which are well resolved by existing instruments. A study of these nebulae, together with those in which any stars at all can be recognized, indicates the probability of an approximately uniform upper limit to the absolute luminosity of stars, in the late-type spirals and irregular nebulae at least, of the order of M (photographic) = $-6.3.$[1] The apparent luminosities of the brightest stars in such nebulae are thus criteria which, although rough and to be applied with caution, furnish reasonable estimates of the distances of all extra-galactic systems in which even a few stars can be detected.

Finally, the nebulae themselves appear to be of a definite order of absolute luminosity, exhibiting a range of four or five magnitudes about an average value M (visual) = $-15.2.$[1] The application of this statistical average to individual cases can rarely be used to advantage, but where considerable numbers are involved, and especially in the various clusters of nebulae, mean apparent luminosities of the nebulae themselves offer reliable estimates of the mean distances.

23

Shown here is the first page of Edwin Hubble's paper "A Relation Between Distance and Radial Velocity Among Extra-Galactic Nebulae," published on January 17, 1929. Here, Hubble first explained that the farther objects in the universe are, the faster they move outward. This ratio of distance to speed is what is known as the Hubble constant. The Hubble constant allows us to calculate the size of the universe. Yet, there is still some uncertainty about the future of the universe. Scientists are divided over whether the universe will continue to expand or reverse direction and begin to grow smaller. If the universe reverses direction, scientists predict that it will end in a collapse called the big crunch. (See pages 53–54 for transcription.)

part of what would develop into the big bang theory. It showed that matter was evenly distributed throughout the universe, as it must be in the aftermath of an explosive creation event.

Using the example of a balloon being blown up at a steady rate, we see that the distance between any two spots on it will increase as the balloon expands. None of the spots are at the balloon's center, but the more the balloon is inflated, the faster the spots will appear to move away from one another. Inflating the balloon can be said to have the same effect on its spots as the expansion of the universe has on the receding galaxies, as shown by Hubble's discovery. The rate of the balloon's inflation is the equivalent of the Hubble constant.

The Hubble constant is expressed mathematically as:

$$H_0 = v/r$$

Hubble constant (H_0) equals a galaxy's red shift, or velocity (v) divided by its distance from Earth (r). As the red shift, or the velocity of a galaxy, increases in the equation, so does its distance. Likewise, as distance increases, so does velocity. The Hubble constant is key in estimating both the age and size of the universe because it expresses the rate at which the universe is expanding.

Hubble originally calculated the numeric value of H_0 to be 93 miles per second (150 kilometers per second) for every 1,000,000 light-years distance. According to modern estimates of H_0, based on more precise measurements, that value has been revised to between 9.3 and 18.8 mi/s (15 and 30 km/s) per 1,000,000 light-years. Hubble therefore believed the universe to be some 2 to 3 billion years old. Modern estimates place the occurrence of the big bang at 12 to 15 billion years ago.

By allowing astronomers to determine the distance to a galaxy, the Hubble constant presents a way to compare the properties of other, more distant galaxies.

Microwaves

Hubble's findings served as the basis for a growing knowledge of the cosmological model of the universe. There was, however, no further evidence to support Hubble's big bang theory beyond his original discovery of the expansion of the universe.

Though Hubble proposed strong evidence that the universe began with the big bang, there wasn't proof of the big bang theory until physicists Arno Penzias *(left)* and Robert Wilson *(right)* of Bell Telephone Laboratories came along. In this photograph, Penzias and Wilson stand next to the antenna they used to detect microwave radiation coming from all corners of the universe. From experiments conducted by physicists Robert Dicke and James Peebles, Penzias and Wilson later learned that the microwaves they detected were radiation that was left over from the earliest moments of the universe. Penzias and Wilson concluded that they had found the first direct evidence that the big bang took place.

Such proof would have to wait until technology caught up with theory. The technology finally came from the work of the American physicists Robert Wilson (1936–) and Arno Penzias (1933–) of the Bell Telephone Laboratories in New Jersey.

In their tests to develop radar and communications links, Wilson and Penzias detected a strong form of radiation called microwaves. Microwaves are part of the electromagnetic spectrum, which includes visible light as well as other forms of radiation such as radio waves, X-rays, and television transmissions, which all have different wavelengths. Microwaves have a longer wavelength than visible light, which is why we cannot see them, but a shorter wavelength than radio waves. No matter which direction Wilson and Penzias pointed the detector in, the excess microwave noise was the same, leading them to believe it was coming from outside the atmosphere.

The time of day or season of the year didn't change the level of noise either. It didn't matter that Earth was continually changing its position through its rotation on its axis and orbit around the Sun. This told them that the noise came from beyond even our solar system and galaxy. Otherwise, the noise would change as Earth's movement pointed the detector in different directions. From the evidence, Wilson and Penzias concluded that this noise was traveling along with us through space and was uniform in all directions.

Meanwhile, at New Jersey's Princeton University, two physicists, the American Robert Dicke (1916–1997) and Canadian James Peebles (1935–) were also looking at microwaves. Their work was based on a theory of one of Alexander Friedmann's students, George Gamow (1904–1968), which stated that the very earliest moments of a universe created by the big bang would have been

Princeton University physicist James Peebles is shown here, standing before an image of the spiral galaxy M100. Peebles collaborated with physicist Robert Dicke to ultimately help discover direct evidence that the big bang took place. Dicke and Peebles theorized that the universe should be filled with microwave radiation if the big bang, in fact, did occur. Dicke and Peebles's work was independent of that of Penzias and Wilson. However, with Dicke and Peebles's microwave theory, Penzias and Wilson realized that their detection of microwave radiation in the universe was the first direct evidence of the big bang.

superdense and incredibly hot. Dicke and Peebles believed we should still be able to see the glow of this infinitely dense and superhot state as light that was only now reaching us. But because of the expansion of the universe across so great a time, any light from about 300,000 years after the big bang would have become so greatly redshifted that it would arrive in the form of microwaves, distributed evenly across the universe.

Physicist Robert Dicke, shown here, was one of the major figures in discovering evidence that the big bang took place. Collaborating with physicist James Peebles, Dicke helped explain that the remnants of the big bang still existed in the form of microwaves. The reason why the remnants would exist in the form of microwaves, Dicke argued, was because they would have been greatly redshifted due to the expansion of the universe—microwaves are a greatly redshifted form of radiation. Dicke's theory turned out to be correct. These microwaves were discovered independently by the scientists Robert Wilson and Arno Penzias. The work of these four scientists supported Hubble's theories of the big bang and the expanding universe.

Hearing of Dicke and Peebles's work, Wilson and Penzias realized they had already found the radiation the two Princeton scientists sought.

Any lingering doubt about the validity of the big bang was all but eliminated in 1970 by the work of two British physicists and mathematicians, Roger Penrose (1931–) and Stephen Hawking (1942–). Penrose had shown that a star collapsing under its own gravity becomes trapped in a region whose surface will eventually shrink to zero size. The collapse compresses all its matter into a region of zero volume, making its density of matter nearly infinite. The result was called a singularity and the area of space it inhabited was called a black hole. Hawking realized that if he reversed the direction of time in Penrose's theory, the collapse became an expansion, possibly mimicking the timeline of the big bang.

In just over forty years, a radical idea that began with Hubble's observation of an expanding universe had made the leap from speculation to solid, scientific fact. British astronomer Fred Hoyle (1915–2001), a lifelong believer in the steady state theory, had mockingly dubbed Hubble's grand creation event the "big bang" on his 1950 British radio program, *The Nature of the Universe*. But his insult helped popularize the theory. No one was mocking the big bang for much longer.

CHAPTER 5

Edwin Powell Hubble's lonely vigils atop Mount Wilson when he was young had made the astronomer a celebrity. The influential and famous made their way to Mount Wilson to meet the man who had opened up the universe. His celebrity rose to even greater heights with the 1931 visit of Albert Einstein, who proclaimed that Hubble's work on the redshift of distant stars enabled him to eliminate the clunky "cosmological constant" from his general theory of relativity. Einstein called the inclusion of this his "greatest blunder."

COSMOLOGY AFTER HUBBLE

Hubble entertained scientists, politicians, and celebrities at both the observatory and with his wife, Grace, at his home in San Marino, California. Among their friends were some of the most famous names in entertainment, from composer Cole Porter to actor Gary Cooper. The couple—who never had any children—traveled extensively to deliver lectures on his work. He was the youngest person ever inducted into the National Academy of Sciences. Then, in 1934, he received an honorary doctorate of sciences degree from Oxford University in England, where he had earned his law degree in 1913.

Hubble was invited to deliver lectures both in America and abroad, meeting with the greatest scientific minds of his day

THE OBSERVATIONAL
APPROACH TO
COSMOLOGY

BY

EDWIN HUBBLE
OF THE MOUNT WILSON OBSERVATORY
CARNEGIE INSTITUTION OF
WASHINGTON

OXFORD
AT THE CLARENDON PRESS
1937

Hubble published *The Observational Approach to Cosmology* in 1937. The title page of that first edition is shown here. In this text, Hubble covered scientific ideas he expressed in his lectures over the years. The publication of the text came after Hubble had made the most important discoveries of his life. Around this time, Hubble also published *The Realm of the Nebulae*. This was one of his most productive periods, in science as well as in other areas. He applied for a job in the military a few years later with the United States' involvement in World War II in 1941. The military was dramatically different from the life he had always known as a curious scientist. (See page 54 for transcription.)

everywhere he went. He published two popular books, *The Realm of the Nebulae* (1936) and *The Observational Approach to Cosmology* (1937), both based on his lectures delivered at Yale University and elsewhere.

Back in Service

When America again went to war in 1941, following the Japanese bombing of the Pearl Harbor Naval Base in Hawaii, Hubble responded as he had to his country's entry into World War I: he applied for a job in the military.

Now fifty-two years old and one of the country's most famous scientists, he was made head of the ballistics research program at Maryland's Aberdeen Proving Ground. The work at Aberdeen was as different as possible from the quiet research of observing the heavens through a telescopic site. It was involved with the science of ballistics, or the motion of projectiles such as bullets and bombs. Ammunition of all sorts was tested and studied to learn how to make the most efficient weapons for the war against the Axis powers (Germany, Italy, Japan, and their allies).

Hubble and his wife were uprooted from their normal academic lives and far from home. Hubble was happy to do his part to restore world peace, but as the war neared its end, with America and its allies on the road to victory, he became anxious to get back to California and his real work, astronomy.

The Palomar Observatory

After the war, the Hubbles returned to Cal Tech. In addition to his regular work at the 100-inch (254 cm) Mount Wilson telescope, Hubble had been involved in the development of an even larger instrument for Cal Tech: the Hale Telescope, which was to be located atop nearby Mount Palomar.

The telescope had been in the works since 1928. Its 200-inch (508 cm), 20-ton Pyrex glass disk mirror was cast at the Corning Glass Works in New York and shipped to Pasadena in 1935 for the long and delicate process of grinding and polishing. The building that was to house this great telescope had moving parts, weighed some 530 tons, and featured a 1,000-ton rotating dome. The building and telescope were nearly complete by 1941, but World War II interrupted the polishing of the mirror. The mirror was not completed and installed into the 55-foot-long (17-meter-long) barrel of the telescope until November 1947. The opening of this mammoth observatory was so momentous that the United States

This 1938 photograph shows the installation of the 200-inch Hale Telescope within the Palomar Observatory. Mount Palomar is located in north San Diego County, California, at an elevation of 5,500 feet (1,676 m) above sea level. The high elevation keeps the telescope above as much city light and air pollution as possible, allowing for better visibility. Though not yet in its final position in this early photograph, the telescope was designed to peer out of the narrow opening shown. To view all corners of the sky, the entire dome itself rotates.

Postal Service created the world's first "space stamp," a 3¢ first-class stamp issued on August 30, 1948.

The Hale Telescope was dedicated on June 3, 1948, and Edwin Hubble was given the honor of processing the first photographic plate. The plate is of a variable nebula, which bears his initials. However, technological problems caused a delay in further observations through the Hale Telescope, during which time Hubble and Grace traveled back to England for more lectures and his election as an honorary fellow of Oxford University's Queen's College.

In July 1949, while on vacation in Colorado, Hubble suffered a heart attack. A second attack followed several days later. Hubble eventually recovered sufficiently to return to work, but always with Grace watching carefully over him. He continued on a modified work and travel schedule, making one final trip to England in April 1953, to address the Royal Astronomical Society and meet the young Queen Elizabeth II.

Hubble made his last visit to Mount Palomar on September 1, spending several hours over the course of three nights viewing the heavens through the great telescope. On September 28, 1953, as he was returning home with Grace, Edwin Powell Hubble passed out in the car. He had suffered a fatal stroke.

The Hubble Space Telescope

Edwin Hubble's legacy in the world of astronomy and physics has proven to be vast and undeniable. His observations of distant spiral nebulae and attempts to measure the distances to galaxies awoke the world to the true vastness of the universe. His name has been attached to many scientific concepts. Perhaps most well known to the world beyond the astronomical community

On August 30, 1948, the United States Postal Service issued a 3¢ first-class "space stamp" upon the opening of the Palomar Observatory. Since then, a line of other stamps dedicated to Hubble and his life's work have been created. Shown here are Edwin P. Hubble commemorative stamps. To the left is young Hubble at the 100-inch (254 cm) Hooker Telescope at the Mount Wilson Observatory. The stamps were issued by the Carnegie Institution, an organization founded in 1902 by steel magnate Andrew Carnegie. The institution was created as a home for exceptional scientists and to promote their work.

Visit World Stamp Expo 2000, Anaheim, California, July 7-16, 2000

Images from the
Hubble Space Telescope
named in honor of
distinguished
American astronomer
EDWIN POWELL HUBBLE

Edwin Hubble

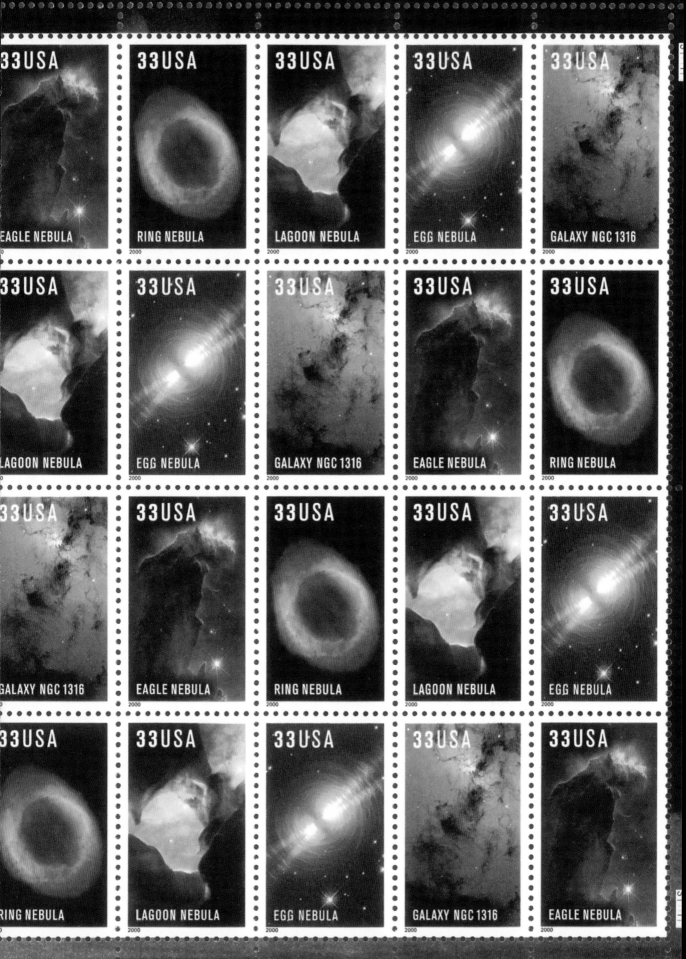

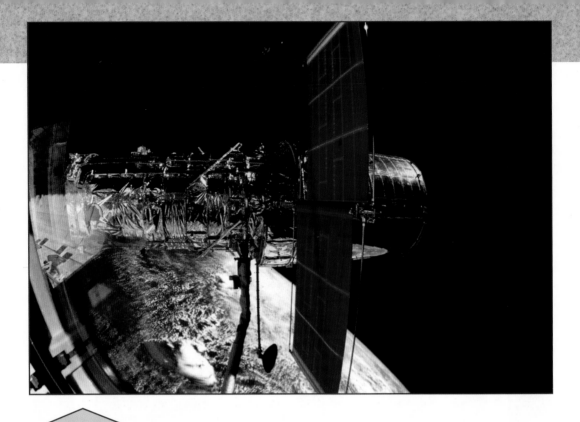

Perhaps the greatest tribute to Edwin Hubble is the telescope that bears his name. The Hubble Space Telescope, shown here in 1990, is the most powerful telescope to date. With it, scientists have been able to see, with near-perfect clarity, corners of the universe never seen before. With all of its success, the Hubble Space Telescope is more than an essential tool for scientific discovery. It is a symbol of Edwin Hubble himself. Without him, we would not have known about the outer reaches of the universe. Without the telescope, we would not be able to see and study these far corners of the heavens today.

and the most fitting tribute to him is the Hubble Space Telescope (HST).

Launched on April 24, 1990, by the space shuttle *Discovery*, the 25,000-pound (11,340-kilogram) HST sits in orbit 375 miles (600 km) over Earth, far above the distorting gasses of the planet's atmosphere. Unlike Earth-based telescopes, the Hubble is not restricted to operation at night or only during clear weather. Its powerful optical devices and precision pointing instruments provide stunning views of the farthest reaches of the universe twenty-four hours a day. It sees billions of light-years farther into

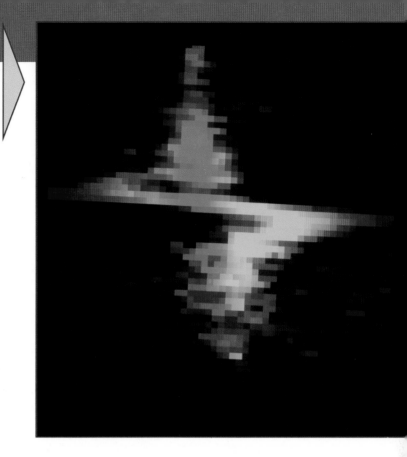

This image of the radiation surrounding a black hole was taken by the Hubble Space Telescope. Using the Doppler effect, the image tells us in which direction the radiation is moving. The material to the left is moving toward us, as is shown by its blueshift. The material to the right is moving away. From this image, we can also tell that the radiation is moving at the phenomenal speed of 248 miles/second (400 km/s) due to the gravity of the black hole. And by calculating its speed, we can tell that the black hole is at least 300 million times more massive than the Sun.

space than was ever thought possible during Hubble's time. With it, scientists can view galaxies as they were during earlier stages of the universe's existence, peering deeper into space and farther back into time than even Hubble had ever imagined.

However, early in 2004, NASA announced the cancellation of further maintenance missions to the space telescope, leading to an early shutdown by 2007 or 2008. With continued maintenance and upgrades, the Hubble could conceivably remain in service for many years, perhaps even beyond the launch, planned for 2011, of the Hubble's replacement. NASA's decision, stemming from budgetary considerations and changes in the space agency's plans, has angered scientists who hope that the Hubble might one day help tear away the veil from the very secrets of the big bang that birthed the universe. This was an event whose existence was first suggested by the work of Edwin Hubble, the remarkable man whose name this telescope now bears.

TIMELINE

1889	— Edwin Powell Hubble is born on November 20, in Marshfield, Missouri.
1897	— Hubble has his first look through a telescope at his grandfather's house.
1905	— Albert Einstein publishes his special theory of relativity.
1906	— Hubble graduates high school in Wheaton, Illinois, and enters the University of Chicago.
1910	— Hubble wins a scholarship to study in England. He studies law for three years at Oxford University.
1912	— Henrietta Swan Leavitt discovers Cepheid variable stars.
1914	— Hubble decides to return to the study of astronomy at the University of Chicago. In August, he is elected a member of the American Astronomical Society.
1915	— Albert Einstein publishes his general theory of relativity.
1917	— Hubble receives his doctorate degree from the University of Chicago and joins the United States Army, where he is made commander of the 2nd Battalion of the 343rd Infantry.
1918	— Harlow Shapley determines the size of the Milky Way galaxy.

1919	—	Hubble leaves the army and returns to the United States, where he accepts a position at California's Mount Wilson Observatory.
1923	—	Hubble discovers a Cepheid variable star in the Andromeda nebula.
1924	—	Hubble marries Grace Burke Leib on February 26. On November 22, an article in the *New York Times* reveals Hubble's discovery of "island universes."
1926	—	Hubble publishes his classification of galaxies in the *Astrophysical Journal*.
1929	—	Hubble lays the groundwork for the big bang theory with the publication of "A Relation Between Distance and Radial Velocity Among Extra-Galactic Nebulae" in the *Proceedings of the National Academy of Sciences*.
1936	—	Hubble publishes his book *The Realm of the Nebulae*.
1937	—	Hubble publishes his book *The Observational Approach to Cosmology*.
1942	—	Hubble is asked to head up the ballistics research program at Maryland's Aberdeen Proving Ground.

1953	— Hubble dies on September 28.
1965	— Robert Wilson and Arno Penzias of Bell Telephone Laboratories discover mysterious microwave "background noise" that Princeton University physicists Robert Dicke and James Peebles determine is a remnant of the big bang.
1970	— Roger Penrose and Stephen W. Hawking mathematically prove the big bang occurred.
1990	— The Hubble Space Telescope is launched aboard the space shuttle *Discovery* on April 24.
2004	— In January, NASA cancels the Hubble Space Telescope's fourth servicing mission, thus cutting short the projected life span of the telescope by several years.

PRIMARY SOURCE TRANSCRIPTIONS

Page 27: From the *New York Times*

WASHINGTON, NOV. 22.—Confirmation of the view that the spiral nebulae, which appear in the heavens as whirling clouds, are really distant stellar systems, or "island universes," has been obtained by Dr. Edwin Hubbell [sic] of the Carnegie Institution's Mount Wilson observatory, through investigations carried out with the observatory's powerful telescopes.

The number of spiral nebulae, the observatory officials have reported to the institution, is very great, amounting to hundreds of thousands, and their apparent sizes range from small objects, almost star-like in character, to the great nebulae in Andromeda, which extends across an angle some 3 degrees in the heavens, about six times the diameter of the full moon.

"The investigations of Dr. Hubbell [sic] were made photographically with the 60-inch and 100-inch reflectors of the Mount Wilson observatory," the report said, "the extreme faintness of the stars under examination making necessary the use of these great telescopes. The revolving power of these instruments breaks up the outer portions of the nebulae into swarms of stars, which may be studied individually and compared with those in our own system.

"From an investigation of the photographs thirty-six variable stars of the type referred to, known as Cepheid variables, were discovered in the two spirals, Andromeda and No. 33, of Messir's great catalogue of nebulae. The study of the periods of these stars and the application of the relationship between length of period and intrinsic brightness at once provided the means of determining the distances of these objects.

"The results are striking in their confirmation of the view that these spiral nebulae are distant stellar systems. They are found to be about ten times as far away as the small Magellanic cloud, or at a distance of the order of 1,000,000 light years. This means that light traveling at the rate of 186,000 miles a second has required a million years to reach us from these nebulae and that we are observing them by light which left them in the Pliocene age upon the earth.

"With a knowledge of the distances of these nebulae we find for their diameters 45,000 light years for the Andromeda nebulae and 15,000 light years for the Messier 33. These quantities, as well as the masses and densities of the systems, are quite comparable with the corresponding values for our local system of stars."

Page 34: From "A Relation Between Distance and Radial Velocity Among Extra-Galactic Nebulae."

Determinations of the motion of the sun with respect to the extra-galactic nebulae have involved a K term of several hundred kilometers which appears to be variable. Explanations of this paradox have been sought in a correlation between apparent radial velocities and distances, but so far the results have not been convincing. The present paper is a re-examination of the question, based on only those nebular distances which are believed to be fairly reliable.

Distances of extra-galactic nebulae depend ultimately upon the application of absolute-luminosity criteria to involved stars whose types can be recognized. These include, among others, Cepheid variables, novae, and blue stars involved in emission nebulosity. Numerical values depend upon the zero point of the period-luminosity relation among Cepheids, the other criteria merely check the order of the distances. This method is restricted to the few nebulae which are well resolved by existing instruments. A study of these nebulae, together with those in which any stars at all can be recognized, indicates the probability of an approximately uniform upper limit to the absolute luminosity of stars, in the late-type spirals and irregular nebulae at least, of the order of M (photographic) = -6.3. The apparent luminosities of the brightest stars in such nebulae are thus criteria which, although rough and to be applied with caution, finish reasonable estimates of the distances of all extra-galactic systems in which even a few stars can be detected.

Finally, the nebulae themselves appear to be of a definite order of absolute luminosity, exhibiting range of four or five magnitudes about an average value M (visual) = -15.2. The application of this statistical average to individual cases can rarely be used to advantage, but where considerable numbers are involved, and especially in the various clusters of nebulae, mean apparent luminosities of the nebulae themselves offer reliable estimates of the mean distances.

Page 42: From *The Observational Approach to Cosmology*

This series of lectures concerns the observational approach to cosmology, to the study of the physical universe. From our home on the earth we look out into the dim distance, back into the dim past, and we strive to imagine the sort of world into which we are born. Observations now range through an immense volume of space: perhaps the nature of the universe may be inferred from the appearance of the sample we explore. Theory presents us with an infinite array of possible universes, logically consistent systems: perhaps our information is now sufficient to identify among them the particular type, or family of types, which includes the actual universe we inhabit. At any rate, astronomy has developed to the point where, for the first time, such attempts are justifiable. Empirical investigations have definitely entered the field of cosmology. Already, certain conclusions can be drawn from the explorations. The long process of elimination and successive approximation has begun.

Cosmology lay for ages in the realm of sheer speculation. Rational arguments were introduced slowly until the critical period just two decades ago. Then theory invaded the field in force, and rapidly exploited the possibilities offered by general relativity. Later still, a dozen years ago, observations crossed the frontiers of the stellar system, and swept out into the universe at large. The observable region of space, our sample of the universe, is now defined, and a preliminary reconnaissance has been completed.

GLOSSARY

astronomer Person who studies distant objects and events outside Earth's atmosphere, such as planets, comets, stars, galaxies, and black holes.

black hole A collapsed star with such strong gravity that not even light can escape it.

blueshift Shortening of a wavelength, either of light or sound, toward the shorter wavelength (blue) end of the electromagnetic spectrum due to the source moving toward the observer.

celestial Of or relating to the sky.

Cepheid variable star A luminous giant star whose brightness varies periodically.

cosmology The study of the large-scale structure and evolution of the universe.

cosmos The universe, from the greek meaning "everything."

Doppler effect The change in length of a wave (light or sound) due to the relative motion of the source toward or away from an observer.

epicycle A circular orbit of a body in the Ptolemaic system, the center of which revolves around another circle.

frequency The number of complete oscillations, or waves, per second for an electromagnetic wave.

galaxy A large body of gas, dust, stars, and planets, held together by their mutual gravitational attraction.

geocentric model Model of the universe with Earth at the center and all other objects moving around it.

gravity A force of attraction between all masses in the universe.

heliocentric model Model of the universe with the Sun at the center and all other objects moving around it.

Hubble constant A measure of the rate of expansion of the universe.

infinite Something that is subject to no limit or end.

light-year The distance that light travels in one year, equaling 5.88 trillion miles (9.46 trillion kilometers).

luminosity A measurement of the amount of radiation a star emits from its surface in one second.

nebula A cloud of gas or dust in space.

parallax The apparent change in location of an object against a background due to the change in position of the observer.

pulsar A rapidly rotating neutron star that emits beams of radiation.

quasar An object that resembles a star but which releases a huge amount of radiation.

redshift Lengthening of a wavelength, either of light or sound, toward the red end of the electromagnetic spectrum due to the source moving away from the observer.

velocity A measurement of the rate of speed in a particular direction.

FOR MORE INFORMATION

American Astronomical Society
2000 Florida Avenue NW, Suite 400
Washington, DC 20009-1231
(202) 328-2010
Web site: http://www.aas.org

Mount Wilson Observatory
c/o CHARA
Georgia State University
MSC 8R0320
One Park Place, Suite 720
Atlanta, GA 30303-3088
(404) 651-2932
Web site: http://www.mtwilson.edu

NASA Headquarters
Information Center
Washington, DC 20546-0001
(202) 358-0000
Web site: http://www.nasa.gov

Space Telescope Science Institute
Office of Public Outreach
3700 San Martin Drive
Baltimore, MD 21218
(410) 338-4444
Web site: http://www.hubblesite.org

Yerkes Observatory
373 W. Geneva Street
Williams Bay, WI 53191
(262) 245-5555
Web site: http://astro.uchicago.edu/yerkes

Web Sites

Due to the changing nature of Internet links, the Rosen Publishing Group, Inc. has developed an online list of Web sites related to the subject of this book. This site is updated regularly. Please use this link to access the list:

http://www.rosenlinks.com/psrsdt/hubb

F OR FURTHER READING

Henbest, Nigel, and Heather Couper. *DK Space Encyclopedia*.
    London: Dorling Kindersley Publishing, 1999.

Hubble, Edwin, and James Gunn. *The Realm of the Nebulae*.
    New Haven, CT: Yale University Press, 1982.

Mitton, Simon, and Jacqueline Mitton. *The Young Oxford Book
    of Astronomy*. Oxford, England: Oxford University Press
    Children's Books, 1996.

Moore, Patrick, and Leif Robinson. *Astronomy Encyclopedia*.
    Oxford, England: Oxford University Press Children's
    Books, 2002.

Ridpath, Ian, and Sir Martin Rees. *The Illustrated Encyclopedia
    of the Universe*. New York: Watson-Guptill Publications, 2001.

Sparrow, Giles, and Robin Kerrod. *The Way the Universe Works*.
    London: Dorling Kindersley Publishing, 2002.

BIBLIOGRAPHY

Christianson, Gale E. *Edwin Hubble: Mariner of the Nebulae.* Toronto: University of Chicago Press, 1996.

Camp, Carole Ann. *American Astronomers, Searchers and Wonderers.* Springfield, NJ: Enslow Publishers, 1995.

Fox, Mary Virginia. *Edwin Hubble, American Astronomer.* New York: Franklin Watts, 1997.

Hawking, Stephen. *A Brief History of Time: The Updated and Expanded Tenth Anniversary Edition.* New York: Bantam, 1998.

Maran, Stephen P. *Astronomy for Dummies.* New York: IDG Books, 1999.

Ryden, Barbara. *Introduction to Cosmology.* Boston: Addison Wesley, 2002.

Zannos, Susan. *Edwin Hubble and the Theory of the Expanding Universe* (Unlocking the Secrets of Science). Hockessin, DE: Mitchell Lane Publishers, Inc., 2003.

PRIMARY SOURCE IMAGE LIST

Cover: Photograph of Edwin P. Hubble, housed at the Mount Wilson Observatory and Observatories of the Carnegie Institution of Washington in Pasadena, California.

Title page: Photograph of Edwin P. Hubble taken on April 27, 1931.

Page 5: Photograph of Yerkes refractor telescope taken on March 6, 1993, by Roger Ressmeyer.

Page 9: Illustrations from *Round the Moon* by Jules Verne, 1870.

Page 11: Photograph of University of Chicago basketball team, 1910. It is housed at the Yerkes Observatory in Williams Bay, Wisconsin.

Page 14: Image of Bug Nebula taken on April 27, 2004 by the Hubble Space Telescope.

Page 16: Illustration titled "Historical Cosmologies" by Johann Georg Heck, from *Bilder Atlas*, 1860.

Page 18: Portrait of Tycho Brahe. It is housed in the Royal Observatory in Edinburgh, Scotland.

Page 22: Photograph of Edwin P. Hubble and Dr. Richard Chase Tolman, located at the Mount Wilson Observatory in Pasadena, California.

Page 23: Photograph of the galaxies M31 and M33. It is located at the Observatories of the Carnegie Institution of Washington in Pasadena, California.

Page 26: Photograph of photographic plate "VAR!," 1923. Housed at the Mount Wilson Observatory and Observatories of the Carnegie Institution of Washington in Pasadena, California.

Page 27: Copy of the *New York Times* article "Finds Spiral Nebulae are Stellar Systems," November 22, 1924. It is located at the New York Times Company in New York.

Page 34: Title page of "A Relation Between Distance and Radial Velocity Among Extra-Galactic Nebulae," by Edwin Hubble, January 17, 1929.

Page 36: Photograph of Arno Penzias and Robert Wilson, May 26, 1993. Housed in the AT&T Bell Laboratories in Holmdel, New Jersey.

Page 38: Photograph of James Peebles, by Roger Ressmeyer, taken on June 9, 1993.

Page 39: Photograph of Robert H. Dicke taken in 1960.

Page 42: Title page of *The Observational Approach to Cosmology* by Edwin P. Hubble. It is housed at the Huntington Library in San Marino, California.

Page 44: Photograph of the Hale Telescope at Mount Palomar, California, taken by Peter Stackpole.

Pages 46–47: Photograph of Hubble commemorative stamps. Housed at the Carnegie Institution of Washington in Washington, DC.

Page 48: Photograph of the Hubble Space Telescope, taken on April 1, 1990.

NDEX

Credits

Cover, pp. 23, 26 courtesy Carnegie Observatories, the Carnegie Institution of Washington; title page, p. 22 © AP/Wide World Photos; pp. 5, 36, 38 © Roger Ressmeyer/Corbis; p. 9 Private Collection/Bridgeman Art Library; p. 11 University of Chicago Photograph; p. 14 ESA/NASA and Albert Zijlstra; p. 16 © Sheila Terry/Photo Researchers, Inc.; p. 18 © Royal Observatory, Edinburgh/Photo Researchers, Inc.; p. 27 © 2004 The New York Times Co., reprinted with permission; p. 29 © Benjamin Bromley/ Photo Researchers, Inc.; p. 34 the Huntington Library, San Marino, CA; p. 39 © Bettmann/Corbis; p. 42 title page from "The Observational Approach to Cosmology" by Hubble, Edwin (1937) by permission of Oxford University Press; pp. 44, 48 Time Life Pictures/Getty Images; p. 49 © NASA/Photo Researchers, Inc.

About the Author

Paul Kupperberg is a freelance writer and editor for DC Comics. He has published more than 700 comic book stories, books, and articles, as well as several years of syndicated *Superman* and *Tom and Jerry* newspaper strips. Paul lives in Connecticut with his wife, Robin, and his son, Max.

Editor: Nicholas Croce; Photo Researcher: Rebecca Anguin-Cohen